AN INTRODUCTION TO WOMEN COMPOSERS

AN INTRODUCTION TO WOMEN COMPOSERS

KAREN L. DUNN

ISBN-13: 9781544753133
ISBN-10: 1544753136
Library of Congress Control Number: 2017904651
CreateSpace Independent Publishing Platform
North Charleston, South Carolina

INTRODUCTION

The purpose of this book is to provide a resource for introducing readers to the stories and compositions of seven women composers. Each of these women lived during one of the six historical musical time periods: medieval, Renaissance, baroque, classical, romantic, and modern.

Each of the women composers is presented with an overview of the musical time period, a short biography, a black-and-white drawing of the composer that can be colored, and a Listening Map for a selected composition. Listening directions are given for the featured pieces of music written by the composers.

All of the selections featured in this book can be purchased and downloaded from iTunes or Amazon, often as a part of a women composer collection, and many can be found on YouTube. The discography page at the end of the book notes a source for each featured selection.

TABLE OF CONTENTS

INTRODUCTION TO THE MEDIEVAL PERIOD
500-1500 CE

The medieval period, or Middle Ages, lasted for one thousand years! This was a time of castles, peasants, monasteries, cathedrals, and crusades. Great leaders, such as Joan of Arc, were part of the Middle Ages, and so were other major events, such as the **Black Plague.**

The Roman Catholic Church was the supreme power during the Middle Ages. It was the stabilizing force in everyday life that kept the community together. The laws and rules of the land were all affected by religion during the Middle Ages. As a result, religious music was important during most of this time period.

A certain type of religious music, **chant**, was created during the Middle Ages. Chant is made up of several short phrases of words set to music. It also consists of a single line of melody, sung in unison, called a **monophonic** melody. Eventually, groups of Catholic monks began to write down these chants. These became known as Gregorian chants, named after Catholic Pope Gregory I.

During the medieval period, many women joined convents. It is difficult to determine how active religious women were as composers because the identities of most medieval women composers remain unknown. The women took vows of humility, which meant that the music was identified only by the composer's first name, her initials, or the city where her convent was located. Hildegard von Bingen, meaning "Hildegard from the town of Bingen," is one of these women composers.

MEDIEVAL COMPOSER: HILDEGARD VON BINGEN
1098–1179

Hildegard von Bingen came from a large family in what is now Germany. She was the tenth child, and although she was bright, she was also frail and sickly. She talked of "holy visions" that she had when she was ill. Due to these visions, when she was eight, her family placed her in the care of a nun, Jutta of Sponheim. She was as an offering to God. Hildegard was raised in the **abbey** and became a nun.

Eventually, Hildegard was appointed the head of the abbey. During this time, she still had "visions of burning lights," accompanied by very bad headaches. She felt that she was in touch with the Bible and other religious works while having these visions. As a result, Hildegard drew **mandalas**: ritualistic geometric designs that are symbolic of the universe. She also wrote a great number of chants about the role of humankind in the divine plan, from creation to redemption.

In her later years, she traveled and preached about the need for changes in the church. She wrote letters to leaders at every level of society. In the last year of her life, she faced the most difficult fight of all. She broke the law by helping to bury a young **excommunicated** man in the sacred grounds of the church. The bishops, the heads of the church, commanded her to dig him up, but she refused. As a result, the abbey was emptied. Eventually, her rights were restored. Just before her death, she wrote a moving letter on the importance of music to a spiritual life. As Joseph Baird (2006,) points out in *The Personal Correspondence of Hildegard of Bingen*, "The body is the vestment of the spirit, which has a living voice, and so it is proper for the body, in harmony with the soul, to use its voice to sing praises to God."(p. 160)

DRAWING OF HILDEGARD VON BINGEN

3

LISTENING MAP FOR "O QUAM MIRABILIS"
("For the Creator")
Composed by Hildegard von Bingen

Listen to the piece, "O Quam Mirabilis" and then listen again following these suggested steps:

1. Think about the mood of the piece.
2. Listen for the voice recognition of males or females.
3. Listen for any instruments that might be accompanying the singing.
4. The song is sung in Latin. Read the lyrics below as your listen to the piece again.
5. Read the English translation on the next page.

O quam mirabilis est presciertia divini pectoris
Que prescivi omnem creaturam.
Nam cum Deus Inspexit faciem hominis
Quem formavit, omnia opera
Sua in eadum forma hominis integra aspexit.
O quam
Mirabilis est Inspiratio que hominem
Sic suscituavit.

Oh,

How

Marvelous

Is the

Fore-

Knowledge

Of the

Divine

Heart

Which

For knew

All

Creation.

For when God looked on the face of man he formed,

He saw all His works whole in that same human form.

Oh,

How

Marvelous

Is the

Inspiration

That

In this

Way

Roused

Man to

Life.

INTRODUCTION TO THE RENAISSANCE PERIOD
1450–1600 CE

After the worst of the Black Plague was finally over, people opened up to human interests and cultural values once again in the era known as the **Renaissance period**. This led to the recovery of the literary and artistic heritage of ancient Greece and Rome. The freedom of individualism, a choice of actions for a person, was encouraged. This spirit influenced the arts, science, architecture, and religion.

Unison or monophonic melodies were being written in the convents and abbeys and for High **Mass**, a Catholic service. A system of music education in the various churches allowed the training of hundreds of singers and composers. Musicians found employment as choirmasters, instrumentalists, singers, instrumental builders, music printers, and organists.

Vocal music with independent lines of melody developed. This new music was called **polyphonic**, and it appeared in motets and madrigals. These songs were short **secular** pieces. **Opera**, sung stories, began in Italy. The development of printing made the distribution of music and the knowledge of music possible for more people.

The rulers of Europe were beginning to see music as a symbol of power and status. The demand for female court musicians increased, and these women earned their living as professional musicians. Parents or private music tutors educated young, upper-class women. For the first time in Western history, men encouraged education for women, although female composers remained in the shadows.

RENAISSANCE COMPOSER: MARGUERITE OF AUSTRIA
1480–1530

Marguerite of Austria was born to Maximillian I, the head of the House of Hapsburg (an Austrian Empire) and his wife, Mary, Duchess of Burgundy. Maximillian and Mary ruled the Low Countries, an area of land in Northwestern Europe. Unfortunately, Mary died at a young age, not long after Marguerite was born. At the age of two, Marguerite was promised to be wed to the son of the king of France, who would become Charles the VIII. Sent to the French court to be raised, she learned literature, art, and music. She wrote poetry and songs.

Sadly, Charles the VIII rejected Marguerite and married another woman. Maximillian I was outraged, and the countries went to war over the annulment of the marriage. Marguerite was then promised to John, the son of Isabella and Ferdinand of Spain. John and Marguerite felt an attachment to each other, and they married in early 1497. John suddenly became ill while they were traveling, and he died that year.

Lastly, Marguerite married Philibert II, Duke of Savoy. She pursued her musical training at court, where she learned to play instruments and sing. She also continued writing poems and songs. Philibert died suddenly a few years later. Marguerite swore off marriage after his death.

The listening selection is a poem that Marguerite set to music. The text is written in French, and the theme is about love. The soprano and tenor voices weave the melody into a **canon**.

DRAWING OF MARGUERITE OF AUSTRIA

LISTENING MAP FOR "POUR UNG JAMAIS"
BY MARGUERITE OF AUSTRIA

Listening Map for "Pour ung Jamais" translates as "For an Eternity"
The lyrics were written by Marguerite of Austria, and the melody was
composed by Pierre de la Rue. This chanson or secular love song is an
example of a very popular style of composition during the renaissance period.
Listen to the piece with your eyes closed the first time. What is the mood?
What feelings do the singers convey? Listen to the piece a second time. Are
the singers accompanied by any instruments? Look up the word *canon* in the
glossary. Does this secular love song create a canon? Does any part of the
melody repeat?

Pour ung jamais
Ung regret me demeure.
Qui, sans cesser,
nuyt et Jour,
A toute'heure,
Tant me tourmente
Que bien vouldroy morir,
Car ma vie' est fors
Seulement languir,
Parquoy fauldra
En la Fin!
Que je meure!

For an eternity
I still have one regret.
Which, without stopping
night and day,
at every hour,
So much torments me
That I would like to die,
Because my life is only
To pine away.
Why does there need to
Be an end?
That I die!

INTRODUCTION TO THE BAROQUE PERIOD
1600-1750 CE

The term **baroque music** refers to a fancy, decorated style of music that existed from around 1600 until 1750 CE. Baroque style also influenced art, clothing, and architecture in Europe.

The main musical composition of this era was opera. Opera consisted of a story or play set to music and performed on a stage. There were costumed, trained singers who sang dramatic *arias*, and a chorus of singers. An orchestra usually played while they sang.

The main instruments of the baroque period were the organ, a feature of many churches, and the **lute**, a pear-shaped string instrument. The recorder was also played at many musical events.

Most women composers came from noble and professional families that could afford private tutors for their daughters. They studied music because it was considered appropriate for well-bred young girls or suitable for girls going into religious life.

Men and women composers of this time period include Johann Sebastian Bach from Germany, George Frederick Handel from Germany, Barbara Strozzi from Italy, and Ann Valentine from England.

BAROQUE COMPOSER: BARBARA STROZZI
1619–1664

Barbara Strozzi was born in Venice, Italy, to Isabella Breiga, an unmarried servant woman. Her mother had worked for Giulio Strozzi, Barbara's father. When Barbara was nine years old, Giulio Strozzi adopted her as his daughter. He was a well-known poet and dramatist. Barbara had a beautiful voice and a great talent in music, and her father encouraged her.

Venice was the operatic capital of Italy at this time, and Barbara studied voice and composition with Francesco Cavalli, a famous opera composer. She became a **virtuoso** singer, although she never publicly performed. Her father founded the *Accademia degli Incogniti* ("The Academy of the Unknowns"). This was a group of free-thinking, prominent writers and composers who significantly influenced the cultural and political life of Venice. Barbara was acknowledged as their hostess and guiding spirit. She had the respect of each of the members.

Barbara Strozzi composed many secular cantatas, which are medium-length pieces for voices and instruments, and **madrigals**. Many of her texts came from poetry about lost love. Her pieces contain contrasts in **tempo** and **dynamics**. She dedicated her works to royalty and wealthy people, in hopes that she would be given the post of court composer, a music writer who is hired by a king to create music at his request. Barbara Strozzi's works stand out because they were published; many other women composers of that time were not as fortunate.

The example of Barbara Strozzi's music is a madrigal. It is sung in Italian. She wrote the melody of this piece.

DRAWING OF BARBARA STROZZI

LISTENING MAP FOR "TRADIMENTOL" BY BARBARA STROZZI

Directions: Listen to the song the first time for the emotion in the singer's voice. Listen to the song again while reading the words. Does the voice match the words? What is an illusion? Are there changes in dynamics? Are there changes in tempo?

Tradimentol ("Betrayal")
Translation by Franca Vanzan

It was my thought that convinced me
That it was a true love,
But in reality it was only a fantasy
Of my imagination,
To render me a prisoner of a sentiment
That wasn't true.
In fact, it was a false love and
Therefore, a false hope.

Love was my body's desire to have someone
Love, caress and talk to me.
Even if I believe in this love with all my soul,
It is always an illusion because it doesn't exist.

Be careful!
If hoping for false love grows in you,
Immediately try to suffocate it,
Because love is so powerful and dangerous,
That it can betray and hurt you!

INTRODUCTION TO THE CLASSICAL PERIOD
1750-1820 CE

The years from 1750 to 1820 CE are known as the **classical period**. Music that was composed during this time period was written with balance and order and with a lighter, clearer texture than baroque music. People believed that this music stimulated the intellect or mind. Strict rules on structure, how the music was put together, were followed.

The orchestra was established during this time. It was not as large as the orchestras of today. Many composers wrote **symphonies**, large pieces of music, for the early orchestras. The **sonata**, a three-part piece, was also popular. Opera and Masses continued to be written and sung during the classical period.

Women's rights in society were being debated, and women were being noticed for their writing or composing. One step forward was the creation of piano, solo, and chamber literature. The **art song**, which is a poem set to music, began at this time. It was called a ***lied*** in Germany, a *melodie* in France, and a *romanza* in Italy. This style of singing could fit comfortably in the smaller performance setting. Composers of the classical period include Wolfgang Amadeus Mozart, Franz Joseph Haydn, and Maria Theresia von Paradis.

CLASSICAL COMPOSER: MARIA THERESIA VON PARADIS
1759–1824

Maria Theresia von Paradis was born in Vienna, Austria. Her father was Joseph Paradis, court councilor to Empress Maria Theresa of Austria, and her mother was Rosalia Maria Levassori della Motta. She was named after Empress Maria of Austria. At the age of three, Maria lost her eyesight. This did not stop her family from giving her a wonderful musical education in piano and singing, with several great teachers. She could memorize well and learned more than sixty piano **concertos**, solo pieces for piano and orchestra.

When Maria was a young lady, her family sought help for her blindness. They hired a famous doctor/hypnotist, Franz Mesmer. Eye treatments enabled Maria to regain a hint of her vision for a time, but this disoriented her so much at the keyboard that her piano playing worsened.

The experience of living away from her family during her treatments gave her the courage to tour the courts of Europe with her mother. While she was on tour, Maria began composing for the first time. She continued her studies. She composed piano concertos and sonatas. She used a handmade composition board with specially shaped pegs for each note value.

Maria and her music were well liked. Mozart even composed a piano concerto for her. This enhanced her playing career, and she produced more original music. Maria toured and composed for many years. Later in her life, she stopped performing and devoted her time to establishing a school for the blind.

The listening selection is a classical piece with a romantic melody. The cello plays the melancholy melody as the piano accompanies quietly.

DRAWING OF MARIA THERESIA VON PARADIS

Listening Map for "Sicilienne" by Maria Theresia von Paradis

Listen to the song with your eyes closed the first time you hear it. Feel the mood of the piece. On the second listening, slowly follow the stream flowing from the top of the page to the bottom with your finger. Does the melody take you there?

INTRODUCTION TO THE ROMANTIC PERIOD
1820-1900 CE

Between the years of 1820 and 1900 CE, music emphasized free expression of imagination and emotion. The musical compositions were rich with **melody** and **harmony**. Instead of writing music that followed definite rules, as in the classical period, the composers were more concerned with how the music made them feel inside.

Composers wrote stories of strange and fantastic characters for the orchestra and opera. Some composers, such as Paul Dukas, began writing **program music** and **tone poems**, such as "The Sorcerer's Apprentice." The piano became the most popular instrument of this period. People wanted to see and hear the best musicians. These musicians were referred to as virtuosos.

Women composers wrote **chamber music**, instrumental music played by a small ensemble. The string quartet is an example of chamber music. Women also composed and sang *lied* as well as other secular vocal music during this time period. Singing gradually became a part of the female middle-class educational programs. Most of the female composers of this period received little music theory and musical composition instruction in school. Women were still discouraged from publishing musical compositions due to society's belief that those pursuits were not "ladylike."

Performances of chamber music and *lied* by women were only given in private homes for family and friends, not the general public. Composers of this period include Franz Liszt of Hungary and siblings Frederic and Fanny Mendelssohn of Germany.

ROMANTIC COMPOSER: FANNY MENDELSSOHN
1805–1847

Fanny and her brother, Felix Mendelssohn, were born into a wealthy family in Berlin, Germany. They had the same musical education, starting with piano lessons given first by their mother, then by famous teachers from France and Germany. At eighteen, Fanny met Wilhelm Hensel. He was a famous artist who traveled and painted portraits all over Europe.

Fanny and Felix were busy composing music. Their parents opened up their house for *musicales*. These were weekly music-sharing times for family and close friends. At that time, men were encouraged more than women to compose and perform in public, although Fanny always played at the *musicales*. She wanted to publish some of her own pieces, but her parents and her brother discouraged her.

Wilhelm returned to Germany, and the two convinced Fanny's parents to let them marry. She traveled to Italy with him but returned home when her mother died, to take care of the family home. Fanny and Wilhelm had one child, Sebastian Ludwig Felix Hensel, named after Johann Sebastian Bach. After several years of composing vocal and instrumental works, Fanny published some of her pieces.

By the age of forty, Fanny had written many kinds of works. She was rehearsing for the family *musicale* when she suffered a stroke and died. Her brother Felix was so depressed that he never recovered, and he died six months later. Fanny wrote about five hundred musical compositions. Some of her unpublished works are housed in the New York Public Library and the Library of Congress.

DRAWING OF FANNY MENDELSSOHN

LISTENING MAP FOR "TRIO FOR PIANO, VIOLIN AND CELLO IN D MINOR, OP. 11" BY FANNY MENDELSSOHN

Directions: Listen to the "Trio for Piano, Violin and Cello in D Minor" the first time and notice the piano, violin and cello coming in and out of the music. Note the theme is written out below and follow the notes up and down as you listen again. The third time you listen to the piece follow the individual instruments as the theme is played on the piano and then played again with all three of the instruments. The fourth time follow the different parts of the music map as the music plays.

Fanny Mendelssohn   Trio for Piano, Violin and Cello in D Minor, Op. 11

The trio is divided into four movements or sections:

I. Allegro molta vivace
II. Andante espressivo
III. Lied: Allegretto
IV. Finale: Allegro moderato

Movement III.–The Lied: Allegretto is the listening selection and is mapped below.

Theme.......... Counter theme..........Theme & Variation.... Counter theme......Counter theme.... Theme...

Theme.. Theme........ Theme..... Theme....

INTRODUCTION TO THE MODERN PERIOD
1900–

At the turn of the century, there were many types of music being composed. Some composers, such as Gustav Mahler, were involved in composing long romantic symphonies. His writing was a bridge between the nineteenth-century tradition and the **modernism** of the early twentieth century. Other composers, such as Claude Debussy, were writing **impressionist** music, where melody was no longer the focus. Instead, the idea was that music evoked a mood in the mind of the listener.

Women performers and composers were establishing their place in the public eye. Margaret Lang and Amy Beach were writing symphonies. The first formal organizations for women composers were established. Constance Runcie, in Indiana, began the Minerva Club. In Ohio, Isabella Beaton opened the Beaton School of Music. The first music festivals for women began in Europe.

There were also composers who were choosing to experiment with new chords and note combinations. **Dissonance**, where the harmony is less important, was the new idea. Sergei Prokofiev's pieces included dissonance, as in the parade theme of "Peter and the Wolf." Composer Arnold Schoenberg believed in abandoning **tonality** by giving the twelve tones of the **chromatic scale** equal importance. This is referred to as **atonal** music. It moves the listener from one level of dissonance to another.

Modernism reigned for fifty years, and composers were obligated, regardless of their specific styles and techniques, to avoid traditional tonal procedures and the comforts of **consonance**. Dissonance was king.

By the 1950s, other kinds of music were evolving. The explosion of technology had a profound impact on music. Instruments were created that employed electromechanical designs and paved the way for electronic instruments and **electronic music**. One early electronic instrument was the Theremin, invented by Professor Theremin. The instrument's controlling section consists of two metal antennas that sense the position of the thereminist's hands and control **oscillators** for the **frequency** of the sound waves with one hand and the **amplitude** with the other.

Magnetic audiotape opened up a new range of sonic possibilities to musicians, composers, producers, and engineers. Tape can be slowed down, sped up, or even run backward during recording or playback, with startling effects. Tapes were joined to form endless loops that would continually play repeated patterns of prerecorded material. Audio amplification and mixing equipment further expanded tape's capabilities as a production medium or form of storage.

Women composers were experimenting with these new ideas. Composer Laurie Anderson used electronic music and invented several devices that she experimented with in her recordings and performance art shows. In 1977, she created a tape-bow violin that uses recorded magnetic tape instead of horsehair in the bow and a magnetic tape head in the bridge of the violin.

Pauline Oliveros was a central figure in the development of electronic **art music**. She was a founding member and director of the San Francisco Tape Music Center in the 1960s.

MODERN COMPOSER: AMY BEACH
1867–1944

Amy Beach was born in New Hampshire. Her mother taught her the piano at an early age. She became a gifted pianist and performed a piano concerto, a piano solo with an orchestra, with the Boston Symphony. When she was twelve, she taught herself composition and started writing songs and longer pieces of music. At eighteen, Amy married Dr. Henry Harris Aubrey Beach, who was twenty-five years her senior. He believed that a husband should support his wife. This worked to her advantage to further her musical composing and publishing. She did not perform many concerts at this time, but she did compose. She honored her husband by publishing all of her pieces under the name Mrs. H. H. A. Beach.

Amy composed in a romantic style because she enjoyed the works of romantic period composers such as Brahms and Beethoven. She also composed a symphony, which was the first symphony ever written by an American woman. Some of the critics were not kind in their reviews. Many people believed this was due to a woman being the composer, not to the work itself.

Both Amy's husband and her mother died in 1910. She wrote fewer compositions and performed in Europe for three years. Amy returned to the United States and divided her time between performing and composing. In 1924, Amy worked to establish the Society of American Women Composers. She helped women composers gain popularity, paving the way for future women composers.

DRAWING OF AMY BEACH

INFORMATION FOR THE LISTENING MAP
FOR "DREAMING" BY AMY BEACH

Directions:
When you are listening to this piece for the first time, just close your eyes and listen. Read over the 6 parts of the listening map explanation before listening to the piece again. On the second listen, follow the melody with the clouds. On the third listening, follow the wave-like harmony of the left hand.

1. There are nine lines of waves and clouds that represent the melody and harmony of this piece.
2. The left land of the pianist creates a wavelike harmony underneath the main melody that is played with the right hand on the piano.
3. The harmony waves stay between two lower notes that move back and forth. The left-hand harmony begins the piece alone.
4. The clouds that slowly drift up and down match the melody that moves between the higher and lower notes on the piano.
5. The shorter clouds represent the short notes of the melody, and the longer clouds are the long notes of the melody.
6. The left-hand harmony plays throughout the piece except for a small part at the end of line 6. The right-hand melody descends alone.

LISTENING MAP FOR "DREAMING" BY AMY BEACH

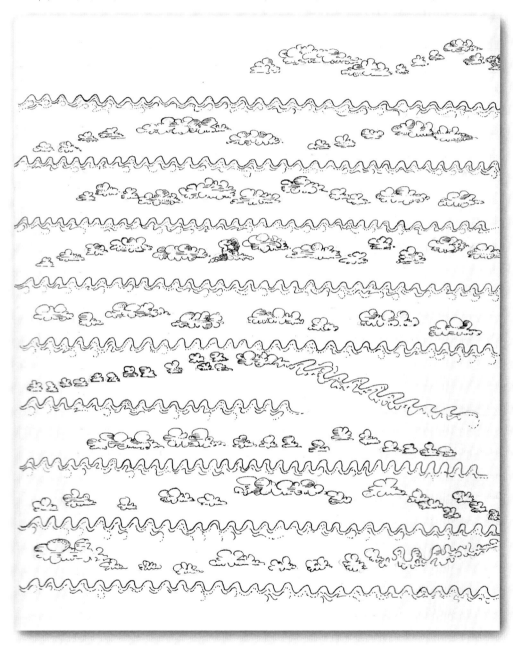

MODERN COMPOSER: PAULINE OLIVEROS
1932–2016

Pauline Oliveros grew up learning about music and piano from her mother and grandmother in Houston, Texas. She took up playing her brother's accordion at the age of thirteen and then taught herself the French horn. However, her first love was the accordion. She decided to become a music composer.

Pauline studied music and the accordion at the University of Houston. In the 1950s, Pauline moved to San Francisco and taught private music lessons; she also worked as an accordion entertainer and a file clerk. She enrolled at San Francisco State College to finish her music degree.

At this time, Pauline became interested in tape-recording the sounds of nature. She also became interested in music **improvisation**, creating music on the spot without planned rehearsal. Along with friends, Pauline set up a studio at the San Francisco Conservatory. They began using tape recorders to augment or change their improvisational music. They created many experimental pieces of music this way. The Tape Music Center became an important part of the San Francisco music scene.

In 1967, Pauline accepted a teaching position at University of California, San Diego. She began to compose pieces using her own unique notation, meditation, and breath cycles. These meditations were influenced by her love of tai chi, a Chinese martial art that she had studied. Her experimental studies grew, and she decided to move to New York to further them.

Upon retirement from teaching, Pauline opened the Deep Listening Institute in the state of New York. The institute is still in operation, and it offers a unique approach to music, literature, listening, and meditation, as well as new technology ideas and healing. People who attend the institute can practice bodywork, such as massage, and mirroring with others, meditation, interactive performances, listening to nature, and listening to their own dreams and thoughts.

Pauline continued to compose new pieces of music. Her compositions range from traditionally notated works for groups to theater to electronic pieces. She performed for audiences all over the world. She always involved the audience, as well as other performers, in the performances. Each performance was never the same because of the improvisations of the audience and the performers.

Pauline was honored in 1985 at John F. Kennedy Center in Washington, DC, and she received a lifetime achievement award for her work from the Society for Electro-Acoustic Music in the United States in 1999.

Pauline continued to explore new technologies. Her most recent idea was the Adaptive Use Musical Instrument, which enables children with extreme physical and cognitive disabilities to play music and improvise with one another.

INFORMATION FOR THE LISTENING MAP FOR "SOUND PATTERNS" BY PAULINE OLIVEROS

In the 1960's Pauline Oliveros found that conventional musical scores did not always work with the sounds she wanted to create. "Sound Patterns" was written as a choral piece that uses phonetic sounds, syllables, and mouth sounds instead of words. The measures were not written in traditional style. Some of the sounds used in the piece correspond to the following four aspects of electronic music:

1. **White noise**: an even mixture of sound waves extending over a wide frequency range. Frequency describes the number of sound waves that pass a fixed place in a given amount of time

2. **Modulation**: an audio signal called the carrier (a wave is in a broadcast frequency band) is varied or changed, and the signal is said to be modulated. The signal whose waveform is being used to control the carrier is called the *modulator* or *program signal*. **Ring or balanced modulation**: a balanced modulator is a device that modifies a signal, usually in the form of an amplitude-modulated (AM) radio signal. It takes the original signal that has both sidebands and a carrier signal, then modulates it so that only the sideband signals come through the output modulator. This creates a balanced signal, as there is less noise because the carrier signal has been removed.

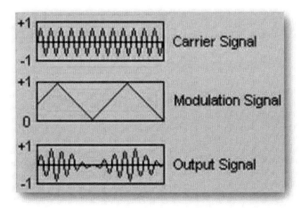

3. **Envelope**: the attack, sustain, and decay of a sound. The combination of these three components of a dynamic musical tone is an element of timbre. Timbre is the distinctive quality, or tone color, of a sound.

    Attack transients consist of changes occurring before the sound reaches its steady-state intensity.

    Sustain refers to the steady state of a sound at its maximum intensity.

    Decay is the rate at which it fades to silence.

    Percussive envelopes are changes in sounds and intensity over time through attack, sustain, and decay.

4. **Filtering** is removing the unwanted frequency or sound waves.

As you listen to "Sound Patterns", notice how it imitates the four aspects of electronic music:

1. The white noise is created vocally through the initial consonant *sh* and other variations, such as *ch*, *ct*, *d*, *h*, *k*, *p*, *s*, *sw*, *t*, *wh*, and *z*.
2. The ring modulation is imitated by rapidly changing the vowel content.
3. The percussive envelopes are lip pops, tongue clicks, snapping fingers, fluttering lips.
4. The filtering is imitated by muting by covering the mouth with one's hand, singing through clenched teeth, and sounding the consonant *m* through tightly closed lips.

This is the **form** or structure of "Sound Patterns":

Exposition-the opening section of the piece where the theme is introduced. (measures 1–12 or lines 1-4)

Development-the central section in which the theme is explored (measures 12–46 or lines 5-8)

Recapitulation-the theme is repeated. (measures 47–59 or lines 9 and 10)

Directions:

Listen for the three parts of the piece. Listen for the four aspects of electronic music. Listening and watching a performance of this piece is recommended. (YouTube does have this option available.)

LISTENING MAP FOR "SOUND PATTERNS" BY PAULINE OLIVEROS
PART 1

<u>Sound Patterns for Mixed Chorus by Pauline Oliveros</u>

Pronounciation: A= father A= at E= she I=bit I= bite
                   O=orb O= old OO=pool OW=owl U=hut
                   Y=bit

Notation: ‖ : stop for a moment   1 4 3 : are meter signatures used
                                 4 4 4   in this piece.

```
4                     1                  4         3
4       p <mf> p       4                  4 Ritard  4    f A tempo
SOP.    SHI-E-I-SH    ‖ REST              REST           (TONGUE CLICK)‖
ALTO    REST          ‖ SHUH              REST           (TONGUE CLICK)‖
TENOR   REST          ‖ SHE-OO-E-OO-E-OO-E-OO  REST      POP LIPS          ‖
BASS    REST          ‖ REST              SOO-SHUH       REST              ‖
```

```
4                     3
4 Slower    fp>   (Hand mute) 4             ff    Faster   (clench teeth)
SOP.    SI----OO----I    ING (GLOTTAL STOP) ZOW    BRRT          ZZZT
ALTO        WA--O (nasal)                   ING (tremolo up) BRRT
TENOR   WA--O-WAO-WAO-WAO (nasal)           SHUNG      R ROLL (TWICE)
BASS UNG (GLOTTAL STOP)        (POP LIPS TWICE)               ZZZT
```

```
3                              4
4    Slower  mf  Faster           ff  4  Faster   <f
SOP.  ZZZT           REST             WHT          PING-------
ALTO  POW WO-WO-WO-WO-WO-WO WHT                    DIT
TENOR PUH                       BBBBBBBBT(LIP FLUTTER(POP LIPS)
BASS     ZZZT  REST                        TOW (CLENCH TEETH)
```

```
4
4    Faster                              f              mf
SOP.    ‖  DIT      OO------------           HUT          PIT
ALTO    ‖  TING------------------------      AN           LA
TENOR   ‖  HO(CLUCK TONGUE) OO- WAO-------(POP LIPS)A HCT HOW-L
BASS    ‖  (POP LIPS) SI-OO--------  SHUH   A---HA---WA--HO-----DOON-
```

```
4
4   Ritard.  f  ff (snap fingers at mouth)    mp
SOP.      CT  ‖ (CLUCK TONGUE)      M---------DIT            SHI
ALTO         DI ‖ (CLUCK TONGUE)    (CLOKE)   DOW-------  SHE-OO-
TENOR HUH     ‖  (CLUCK TONGUE)         (CLOKE)    SI----------------
BASS --------  ‖  (CLUCK TONGUE)    SHI------------------------ OON-----
```

Sound Patterns by Pauline Oliveros

```
4
4      faster  f
SOP. ---- CHUH (POP LIPS) DI      ||    HIT        HAH---PLING      R ROLL-
ALTO --- CHUH (POP LIPS)          ||    PIP      INK    REE-------
TENOR-- CHUH    WA-               ||    ---- SI-ZOONK DIT                R ROLL-
BASS----HUN                       ||    DRRUMP PAH--------SOOT    TOP HAR
```

```
4                                                                3
4      sfз    ff Faster      ff              mf    sfз          4
SOP.        DRRUMP ET     HT    POP        D-DUP  THU           REST
ALTO             SOOT     HT     HIT       PIN------WHT THU     REST
TENOR  ET CHA             HT              DUP      WITE         KEE-------K
BASS       BRRRT          HT BR  RRRUM------  ---WHT            REST
```

```
3
4              mf          f          f < >   slower
SOP.    REST    BIT       GUH        O---------------------    REST
ALTO    KA-----          WHEEK  GOT      BBBBT (FLUTTER LIPS)          AH
TENOR  REST      DITE              REST          AH-----------------
BASS    THUNG---------   KUH       REST                 REST
```

```
3
4                               mp <       >                       f
SOP.     BBBB  FLUTTER) AH-------------    M------------------------    M--
ALTO------------------------    M-------------------------    M----------------
TENOR--- BBBB (FLUTTER)  REST CLENCH TEETH  OO E OO E     M----------
BASS  AN (NASAL)---- REST        (CLENCH TEETH--------------------OO E---
```

```
3
4      >  <  >    <  p    <   pp                accelerando
SOP.   OO   E    OO (Clench teeth M (Close lips)  M-------------------
ALTO  M-----------------------OO------         REST       M(Close lips)----
TENOR---------------M (CLOSE LIPS)------------   OO E OO E--------  REST
BASS------- M-------------OO-------------E--------------------       REST
```

ABOUT THE AUTHOR

Karen L. Dunn has made a career of teaching music. After graduating from Sacramento State College, she earned her master's degree in education from La Verne University.

Now retired, Dunn continues her musical endeavors through singing with the Sacramento Women's Choir and playing piano in a performing trio called the Middle Sisters.

DISCOGRAPHY

All of the following selections can be purchased on iTunes.

Medieval Selection:
"O Quam Mirabilis" ("For the Creator") by Hildegard von Bingen
Performed by Anonymous 4
The Origin of Fire: Musical Visions of Hildegard von Bingen

Renaissance Selection:
"Por Ung Jamais" by Marguerite of Austria
Performed by Corvina Consort
Chansons from the Album of Marguerite of Austria

Baroque Selection:
"Tradimentol" by Barbara Strozzi
Performed by Catherine Bolt
To the Unknown Goddess: A Portrait of Barbara Strozzi
Carlton Classics

Classical Selection:
"Sicilienne in E Flat Major" by Maria Theresia von Paradis
Performed by Jacqueline du Pre and Gerald Moore
A Lasting Inspiration

Romantic Selection:
"Trio for Piano, Violin and Cello in D Minor, Op. 11" by Fanny Mendelssohn
Performed by the Macalester Trio
Chamber Works by Women Composers 1991

Modern Selections:
"Dreaming" by Amy Beach
Performed by Alan Feinberg, piano
The American Romantic 1991
London Records

"Sound Patterns" by Pauline Oliveros
Performed by Alvin Lucier and the Brandeis University Chamber Chorus
Extended Voices

GLOSSARY

Abbey: a dwelling place of a community of nuns and monks, bound by vows to a religious life and often living in partial or complete seclusion. Monasteries are referred to as abbeys when they are independent, are self-sufficient, and have a certain number of nuns or monks. The head of the abbey is either the abbot or abbess. An abbess must be at least forty years old, have been a nun for ten years, and be elected by the secret votes of the nuns belonging to the community.

Accompaniment: vocal or instrumental part of a song that supports a solo or group of singers or instrumentalists. Example: person playing piano for a singer.

Amplitude: a measurement of the size of each individual sound wave according to its "height" or "intensity" rather than its length. This is the amplitude of the wave, and it determines the loudness of the sound. Example: sound waves.

Art music: serious music written by a composer rather than music passed on by oral tradition, such as a folk song.

Art song: a song written by a composer that is sung in public for an audience, usually with a piano **accompaniment**. The song is set or written to a poem.

Atonal: a twentieth-century term used to define music that seems to lack a clear sense of tonality. In tonal music, a tone or note functions like a center of gravity, and the other tones in the **major scale** or minor scale are "attracted" to it in varying degrees of strength. In atonal music, there is no gravity. The composer can use any of the twelve tones in the chromatic scale in any way he or she chooses. This music can be described as free and clashing. Example: In 1908, Arnold Schoenberg, the father of atonal music, composed his pieces using all of the **keys** of the chromatic scale in the same order each time they were played.

Baroque music: a style of European music written from 1600 to 1750. Baroque period composers created the idea of tonal music. Composers and performers made changes in musical notation, such as adding dynamics to their pieces that created contrasts of loudness and softness. Baroque music expanded the size, range, and complexity of instrumental performance. This period used opera, concerto, and sonata forms of music. Composers wrote melodies that were more ornate and exaggerated. Example: baroque music had many trills; a trill is a rapid alternating of played notes that sit next to each other, such as C, D, C, D, C, D.

Black Plague or Black Death: in the Late Middle Ages (1340–1400 CE), it was the deadliest contagious disease; it spread from Asian fleas to rats, to people on ships, and then to others in countries all over Europe. It killed over one hundred million people or a third of the population. The disease, which still exists in some countries today, is now called the bubonic plague.

Canon: a piece of music in which the same melody is begun in different parts, one after another, so that imitations of the melody overlap

Chamber music: instrumental music played by a small group, with one player to a part. Example: a string quartet is made up of two violins, one viola, and one cellist.

Chanson: a French secular and **lyrical** song. The earliest chansons were the story poems performed to simple monophonic melodies by singers and minstrels.

Chant: a short musical, lyrical passage in two or more musical phrases used for singing, usually in unison. Chants were originally sung in Latin.

Chromatic scale: Western music is based on this scale of twelve notes with half steps or intervals. If a person playing the piano plays all the black and white keys of an octave (eight tones) in an ascending or descending order, the result is a chromatic scale. Example: C, C#, D, D#, E, F, F#, G, G#, A, A#, B, C.

Classical period: music produced in the Western world between 1750 and 1820. This period introduced the importance of clarity and form in music composition. The **sonata form** was established, and the modern concerto, symphony, trio, and quartet were developed. A simpler texture in composition, **homophonic**, began during this period. Two composers from this era are Mozart and Beethoven.

Concerto: a musical composition for a solo instrument or instruments accompanied by an orchestra. Example: solo piano player and an orchestra.

Consonance: a combination of tones regarded as pleasing and harmonious.

Dissonance: a disagreeable combination of tones that suggests tension and requires resolution.

Dynamics: the loudness and softness of the music; a part of musical expression. Dynamic markings are usually written into the music using abbreviations for Latin and Italian words. Example: the Italian word *forte*, meaning "loud," is written in the music as *f*.

Electronic music: music produced or changed by an electronic process or specific electronic musical equipment or instruments. Example: electric guitar.

Excommunicate: to not allow a person to continue being a member of the Roman Catholic Church.

Form: the arrangement of various parts of a musical piece and the structure of a piece of music. Example: in AB form, also called binary form, there are two different parts of a song.

Frequency: the rate at which a vibration occurs in a sound wave or in an electromagnetic field (radio waves and light), usually measured per second.

Galliard: lively dance for two people, with complicated turns and steps.

Harmony: the combination of notes sounded simultaneously that create an agreeable sound.

Homophonic: a melody that is played on top of harmonizing chords played by supporting instruments or voices underneath. Example: a choir singing in parts.

Impressionism: a style of writing from the early twentieth century that emphasizes the sense of a piece's topic or mood rather than the pattern of the notes or the strength of the beat. Traditional harmony was avoided, and **whole-tone scales** were used. Example: the composer Debussy and his piece "La Mer."

Improvisation: to make, compose or perform with little or no preparation.

Key: a specific group of notes that relate to a single note called a **tonic** or home tone.

Lied (pronounced *leed*): a type of German song that began during the romantic period, usually written for solo voice and piano accompaniment.

Lute: plucked stringed instrument with a long neck and a pear-shaped body.

Lyrical: song using words or lyrics along with the melody of the song.

Madrigal: an unaccompanied part song for two or three voices that follows a strict poetic form. The text is secular. It developed in Italy in the late thirteenth century.

Major scale: **scale** refers to the basic order of the group of notes in a key. The major scale is a series of notes that go in an ascending and descending manner; it is the foundation from which all other scales are formed.

The C major scale begins with C and ends with C. The notes on a major scale can be numbered from one to eight with **solfege**: do, re, mi, fa, sol, la, ti, do.

Mandala: meaning "circle" in Sanskrit, the ancient language of India. Mandalas are sacred circles that have been used for meditation in the Indian as well as other religions. People create and look at mandalas to center the body and mind.

Mass: Catholic Church ceremonial service spoken in Latin. The structure of the Mass has four parts:

Rites—greeting, blessings, and readings
Liturgy of the Word—readings, prayers
Liturgy of the Eucharist—Lord's Supper
Concluding Rite—blessing

Melody: a succession of single tones that create an idea or tune.

Modernism: a style or movement in music that aims to break with classical and traditional forms; began in the twentieth century.

Monophonic or monody: music made up of a single line of melody that is sung or played without any accompaniment.

Movement: a principal division of a longer musical work.

Opera: a sung story that is acted out on a stage with musical performers in costumes and makeup. Operatic characters sing their lines. The text of an opera is called the libretto. Arias are solo pieces written for main characters, which focus on the character's emotion. Words that are sung in a conversational style are called the recitative.

Oscillator: a device for generating oscillating or moving electric currents by non-mechanical means.

Polyphonic: music consisting of two or more independent and harmonious melodies. Example: the *Music Man* selection "Talk-A-Little/Goodnight Ladies."

Program music: one-**movement** music that is intended to evoke images or events.

Renaissance period: European musical period from 1400 to 1600. There was a revival of art and music that brought people back to human interests and cultural values. An interest in language created a close relationship between words and music, and composers began to write music with deeper meaning. Opera began in Italy. Sacred choral music still remained important, but composers started to take a much greater interest in composing **secular** music. Purely instrumental music—**galliards**—and other secular music came into their own, encouraging music making based on singing, dancing, and plucked keyboard instruments. Renaissance music melodies were written with polyphonic texture.

Scale: a set of musical notes in which each note is higher or lower than the previous one by a particular amount, such a half step. Examples: chromatic scale.

Secular: not connected with religion.

Solfege: French term for the main system of assigning the notes of a scale to a particular syllable instead of a letter. Example: do, re, me, fa, sol, la, ti, do.

Sonata: a musical composition of three or four movements of contrasting forms.

Sonata form: important principle of musical form from the classical period that was carried into the twentieth century of modern music. It is a longer orchestral or chamber piece that is usually composed of three sections:

* *Exposition*—where the primary thematic material for the movement is presented.
* *Development*—starts in the same key as where the exposition ended and may move through many different keys during its course. It will usually consist of one or more themes from the exposition that are altered and may include new themes.
* *Recapitulation*—an altered repeat of the exposition that consists of the following:
  ○ First subject group—the highlight of a recapitulation, usually in exactly the same key and form as in the exposition.
  ○ Transition—an introduction of new material and a short additional development section called the secondary development.
  ○ Second subject group—usually the same form as in the exposition, now in the home key, which sometimes involves a change of mode from major to minor or vice versa.

Symphony: large-scale work with for a full orchestra written with three or four movements, each with a different mood and tempo. One of these movements is in sonata form. Example: Beethoven's Fifth Symphony.

Tempo: the speed at which a piece of music is or should be played.

Tonality: character or mood of a piece of music as determined by the key in which it is played or the relationship between the notes of a scale or key.

Tone poem: piece of orchestral music, usually in one movement or section, that is written on a descriptive theme.

Tonic: the primary pitch or frequency of the key in the music.

Virtuoso: a person highly skilled in music who performs for others.

Whole-tone scale: succession of notes with the interval of a whole step between each note. Examples: C, D, F, G, A, C or C, E, E, F#, G#, A#, C.

REFERENCES

Baird, J. *The Personal Correspondence of Hildegard of Bingen.* Oxford: Oxford University Press, 2006.

Fuller, S. *The Pandora Guide to Women Composers: Britain and the United States: 1629–Present.* London: Harper Collins, 1994.

Hass, J. *An Acoustics Primer.* Bloomington: Center for Electronic and Computer Music, Indiana University, 2012.

Jezic, D. P., and E. Wood. *Women Composers: The Lost Tradition Found,* 2nd ed. New York: Feminine Press, 1988.

Kengall Wolff, C. *Stories of Women Composers for Young Musicians.* Takoma Park, MD: Toadwood, 1993.

Landon, H. C., and J. Norwich. *Five Centuries of Music in Venice.* London: Thames and Hudson Limited, 1991.

Llewellyn, S. *Amy Beach and Judith Lang Zaimont: A Comparative Study of Their Lives and Songs.* Tempe: Arizona State University, 2008.

Miesel, S., January 25, 2012. "Hildegard of Bingen: Voice of the Living Light." *The Catholic World Report.* Retrieved from http://catholicworldreport.com

Nichols, Janet. *Women Music Makers: An Introduction to Women Composers.* New York: Walker & Company, 1992.

Patton, S. *Musicians: A Teaching Guide for Gifted/Talented Students.* Tucson, AZ: Zephyr Press, 1976.

Picker, M. *The Chanson Albums of Marguerite of Austria.* Los Angeles: University of California Press, 1965.

Plantamura, C. *Women Composers.* San Diego: University of California, 1988.

Reich, Susanna. *Clara Schumann: Piano Virtuoso.* Boston: Clarion Books, 1999.

Sadie, Julie Ann, and Rhian Samuel, eds. *The Norton Grove Dictionary of Women Composers.* London: Macmillan Press Limited, 1995.

Zach, Miriam. *For the Birds: Women Composers.* Vol. 1 of *Music History Speller.* Ames, IA: Culicidae Press, 2006.

Made in United States
North Haven, CT
18 May 2022